SANJEEV KAPOOR

The Party Food Cookbook

In association with Alyona Kapoor

Popular Prakashan
www.popularprakashan.com

Published by
POPULAR PRAKASHAN PVT. LTD.
301, Mahalaxmi Chambers
22, Bhulabhai Desai Road
Mumbai - 400 026
for KHANA KHAZANA PUBLICATIONS PVT. LTD.

First Published 2013
First Reprint 2014

(4319)
ISBN: 978-81-7991-760-2

Design: Anjali Sawant
Photography: Bharat Bhirangi, Swapnil Naik and Vikas Shinde

PRINTED IN INDIA
by Saurabh Printers Pvt. Ltd.
A-16, Sector 4, Noida

Contents

Main Course

Accompaniments

Desserts

Author's Note

A party is all about entertaining friends and family. There is nothing more enjoyable than cooking up a meal for family and friends.

However, for many entertaining at home can be a bit of a chore. Today's fast pace of life often prompts one to take the easy way out: order food from a restaurant. A perfectly good option, but we all know, a bit of a compromise on the real thing: entertaining at home with all the personal care that goes into a home-cooked meal, served in the comfort of one's own home.

Colour, texture, variety, taste, and presentation all play a part in one's selection of the best menu to put together for any occasion, but nothing can replace the personal touch.

In *The Party Food Cookbook* I have introduced you to a mouth-watering selection of Indian and international dishes. Wow your guests with refreshing Virgin Pina Colada, crunchy Sichuan Vegetable Fingers, Smoked Chicken and Fruit Salad, spicy Fish Tikka Achaari, silky smooth Paneer Kaliya and luscious Kesari Phirni, to name a few.

Remember, the simplest dish can be made special and elegant not only by the presentation, but also by the warmth with which it is offered.

Happy Cooking!

Coconut Refresher

2 whole tender coconuts
2 apples, peeled, cored, and roughly chopped
8 tablespoons sugar syrup
2 tablespoons lemon juice
4 apple fans, for garnishing

Chill the whole tender coconuts thoroughly. Slice off the tops, drain the water and scoop out the flesh.

Blend the coconut water with the coconut flesh, apples, sugar syrup and lemon juice in a blender until smooth.

Pour into individual glasses. Decorate with apple fans and serve chilled.

Note: Tender coconut water is a natural, safe and a hygienic drink recommended for maintaining electrolyte balance and is also a good aid to treat dehydration.

Party Punch

4 tablespoons rose syrup
2 cups orange juice
2 cups mango juice
4 scoops vanilla ice cream
1 cup ice cubes

Pour one tablespoon rose syrup into each glass and swirl to form a design. Place the glasses in the refrigerator to chill.

Process the orange juice, mango juice and vanilla ice cream with the ice cubes in a blender till smooth.

Pour the prepared punch into the rose syrup-lined glasses and serve immediately.

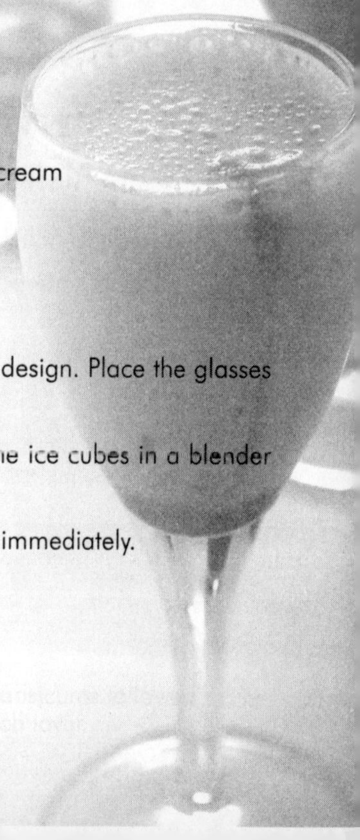

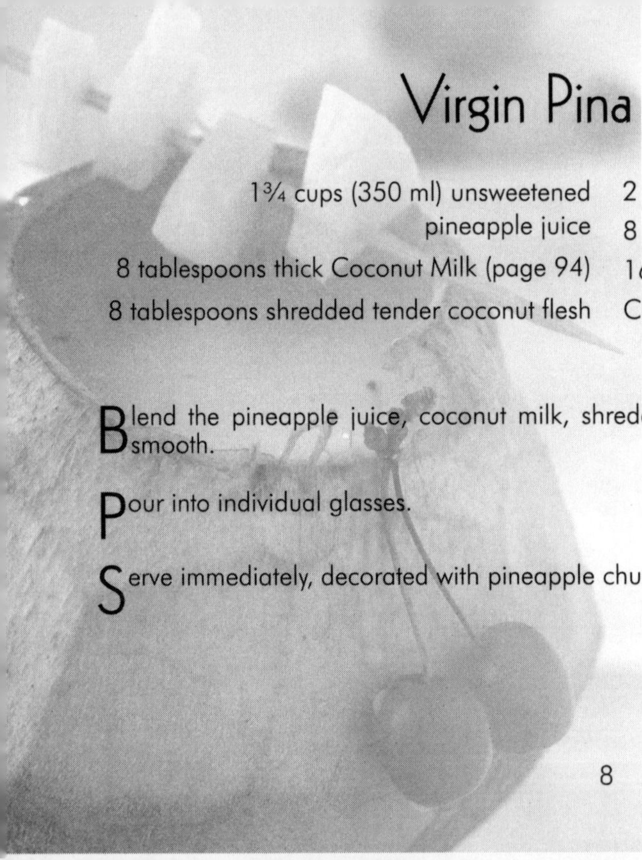

Virgin Pina Colada

- 1¾ cups (350 ml) unsweetened pineapple juice
- 8 tablespoons thick Coconut Milk (page 94)
- 8 tablespoons shredded tender coconut flesh
- 2 cups vanilla ice cream
- 8 tablespoons chopped pineapple chunks
- 16-20 tinned cherries
- Crushed ice

Blend the pineapple juice, coconut milk, shredded coconut, vanilla ice cream and ice till smooth.

Pour into individual glasses.

Serve immediately, decorated with pineapple chunks and cherries.

Virgin Pina Colada

Green Lady

Green Lady

- 8 tablespoons *khus* syrup
- A pinch of salt
- 2 tablespoons lemon juice
- 4 glasses lemonade
- 4 lemon slices
- Crushed ice

Mix together the *khus* syrup, salt and lemon juice.

Add the crushed ice and lemonade and stir well.

Garnish with a slice of lemon and serve chilled.

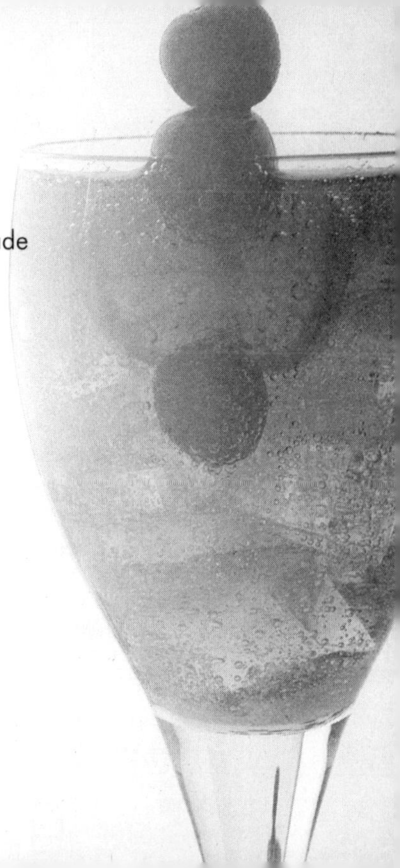

Mushroom Soup With Almonds

400 grams fresh button mushrooms, chopped
30 almonds
1 tablespoon butter
2 medium onions, finely chopped
5 cups milk
Salt to taste
White pepper powder to taste

Blanch the almonds in one cup of hot water. Drain and peel; crush twenty almonds coarsely and cut the rest into thin slivers.

Heat the butter in a non-stick pan; add the onions and mushrooms, and sauté till they soften. Cool and process in a blender to make a smooth purée.

Transfer the purée to a non-stick pan; add the milk and mix well. Bring to a boil over medium heat. Add the crushed almonds, salt and pepper powder, and stir to mix.

Serve piping hot, garnished with the almond slivers.

Chef's Tip: Do not wash or soak the mushrooms. Wipe them with a damp cloth.

Balinese Vegetable Soup

225 grams French beans, cut into ½-inch pieces
Salt to taste
2 cups thick Coconut Milk (page 94)
1 garlic clove
2 fresh red chillies, chopped
4 almonds
½ tablespoon coriander powder
2 tablespoons oil
1 medium onion, sliced
2 bay leaves
1⅓ cups bean sprouts
2 tablespoons lemon juice

Cook the French beans in six cups of boiling salted water for three to four minutes. Drain and reserve the cooking liquid.

Skim off four tablespoons of coconut cream from the top of the coconut milk and reserve.

Grind the garlic, fresh red chillies, almonds and coriander powder to a paste.

Heat the oil in a non-stick wok; add the onion and sauté till translucent. Drain and set aside.

To the same oil, add the ground paste and sauté without browning for about two minutes. Add the reserved cooking liquid and coconut milk. Bring to a boil and add the bay leaves.

Cook, uncovered, for fifteen to twenty minutes.

Just before serving, stir in the beans, sautéed onion, bean sprouts, reserved coconut cream and lemon juice. Adjust the salt and serve immediately.

Sweetcorn Soup With Mixed Vegetables And Tofu

150 grams cream-style sweetcorn
½ cup sweetcorn kernels
¼ small cabbage, chopped
¼ medium carrot, chopped
100 grams tofu (bean curd), cut into ½-inch pieces
2 tablespoons oil
4-5 cups Vegetable Stock (page 95)
Salt to taste
¼ teaspoon white pepper powder
½ tablespoon sugar
¼ teaspoon MSG (optional)
3 tablespoons cornflour, mixed in ½ cup water
1 spring onion green stalk, chopped

Heat oil in a non-stick wok. Add corn kernels, cabbage and carrot. Stir-fry for two minutes. Stir in vegetable stock and bring to a boil.

Mix in the cream-style sweet corn and continue to cook for two to three minutes.

Add salt, white pepper powder, sugar and MSG.

Add the tofu and stir in cornflour mixture, cook on high heat for one minute or until the soup has thickened, stirring continuously.

Serve piping hot, garnished with chopped spring onion green stalk.

(image on page 19)

Summer Tomato Pasta Salad

10-12 cherry tomatoes, halved
1½ cups penne pasta (quill-shaped pasta)
Salt to taste
¼ medium broccoli, separated into small florets
½ teaspoon sugar
15-20 basil leaves
10-12 black peppercorns

2 tablespoons olive oil
150 grams cottage cheese, cut into 2-inch long strips
1 tablespoon vinegar
1 teaspoon caster sugar
2 tablespoons pine nuts/or chopped walnuts (optional)

Cook the pasta in five to six cups of salted boiling water till *al dente* (cooked, but still firm to the bite). Drain, refresh in cold water and spread on a large plate to cool.

Boil the broccoli with salt and sugar for two to three minutes. Drain, refresh in cold water and set it aside.

Reserve three to four basil leaves for garnishing and crush the rest with the peppercorns and one tablespoon of olive oil with a mortar and pestle. Stir the remaining olive oil into the paste.

In a large bowl combine pasta, cherry tomatoes, broccoli, cottage cheese, prepared paste, vinegar, caster sugar and salt. Toss well to mix.

Transfer the salad onto a serving dish, garnish with the remaining basil leaves and pine nuts or walnuts and serve immediately.

Note: You can also use large tomatoes cut into quarters in place of cherry tomatoes.

(recipe on page 15)

Sweetcorn Soup with Mixed Vegetables and Tofu

Smoked Chicken and Fruit Salad

Smoked Chicken And Fruit Salad

225 grams boneless chicken breast
Salt to taste
2 teaspoons lemon juice
75 grams seedless green grapes, peeled and halved
1 pear, peeled, cored and sliced
25 grams walnut halves
4 iceberg lettuce leaves, shredded
2 celery stalks, chopped
1 red capsicum, seeded and sliced
Few fresh tarragon sprigs

Dressing

2 tablespoons yogurt
2 tablespoons Mayonnaise (page 94)
2 tablespoons grated cucumber
1 teaspoon grated onion
½ teaspoon chopped fresh tarragon
Salt to taste
Black pepper powder to taste

Marinate the chicken breast with salt and lemon juice for about half an hour. Grill till both sides are evenly cooked and golden. Set aside to cool. Cut into strips.

In a large bowl, combine the chicken strips with the green grapes, pear, walnuts, lettuce, celery and red capsicum.

In a separate bowl, combine the yogurt, mayonnaise, cucumber, onion, tarragon, salt and pepper powder.

Just before serving, spoon the dressing over the salad ingredients and toss well to mix.

Garnish with a few sprigs of fresh tarragon and serve.

Dhaniya Adrak Champe

500 grams lamb chops

Marinade

½ small bunch (25 grams) fresh coriander
2 inches ginger
2 tablespoons chopped unripe papaya
½ teaspoon soda bicarbonate
10 fresh spinach leaves
4 green chillies
½ cup drained yogurt
1 tablespoon vinegar
1½ inches ginger, finely grated
5-6 black peppercorns, crushed
2 tablespoons roasted gram flour
Salt to taste
1 tablespoon oil
4 tablespoons melted butter

Pat the lamb chops dry with a kitchen towel. Flatten them with a rolling pin or with the back of a knife. Prick all over with a fork.

Grind the fresh coriander, ginger, papaya, soda bicarbonate, spinach and green chillies to a fine paste.

Place the ground paste in a bowl; add the yogurt, vinegar, grated ginger, crushed peppercorns, roasted gram flour, salt and oil and mix well. Add the mutton chops, mix and set aside in a refrigerator to marinate overnight.

Preheat the oven to 180°C/350°F/Gas Mark 4 or heat a gas tandoor over a medium heat.

Place the marinated chops on a greased wire rack or grill and rub them with the marinade left in the bowl.

Grill the chops for twenty minutes, turning once in between. Baste with butter and grill for another fifteen minutes or till tender.

Serve with Mint Chutney (page 94).

Makai, Badam Aur Akhrot Ki Tikki

- 1½ cups (300 grams) corn kernels, boiled and ground
- 20 almonds, blanched, peeled and ground
- 16 walnut halves, chopped
- 200 grams lotus roots
- 2 tablespoons oil + for shallow-frying
- 1 teaspoon caraway seeds
- 1 teaspoon red chilli powder
- 1 teaspoon black pepper powder
- 1 teaspoon fennel powder
- 1 teaspoon *garam masala* powder
- 1 teaspoon *chaat masala*
- 100 grams cottage cheese, grated
- Salt to taste
- ½ cup grated processed cheese
- 1 tablespoon lemon juice
- 1 inch ginger, chopped
- 2 tablespoons chopped fresh coriander
- 24 raisins, chopped

Clean and scrape lotus roots. Grate and boil until soft. Drain and squeeze out excess water. Grind to a paste. Set aside.

Heat two tablespoons oil in a non-stick *kadai*, add caraway seeds and sauté till fragrant. Add corn paste, almond paste, lotus root paste and sauté till the mixture dries up.

Add chilli powder, pepper powder, fennel powder, *garam masala* powder and *chaat masala* and mix well. Add cottage cheese and salt and mix well. Cook till the mixture leaves the sides of the *kadai*.

Remove from heat, add processed cheese, lemon juice, ginger and chopped coriander. Cool the mixture.

Divide into twenty equal balls. Stuff the balls with walnuts and raisins and shape them into *tikki*.

Shallow-fry the *tikki* in a non-stick frying pan using a little oil. Drain and place them on an absorbent paper.

Serve hot with Green Chutney (page 94).

Malai Khumb

- ⅓ cup cream
- 200 grams large fresh button mushrooms, trimmed
- 2 teaspoons garlic paste
- 1 teaspoon green chilli paste
- 8-10 cashew nuts, ground
- 1 teaspoon green cardamom powder
- 3 tablespoons grated processed cheese
- Salt to taste
- 2 tablespoons melted butter
- 1 teaspoon *chaat masala*
- 1 tablespoon lemon juice

Mix together the garlic paste, green chilli paste, ground cashew nuts and cardamom powder in a bowl. Add the cream, cheese and salt and mix. Add the mushrooms, mix thoroughly and set aside, preferably in a refrigerator, for at least half an hour.

Preheat the oven to 200°C/400°F/Gas Mark 6.

Thread the marinated mushrooms onto skewers and cook in the preheated oven or in a moderately hot *tandoor* for about three to four minutes, turning them occasionally. Brush the cooked mushrooms with butter and cook again for three or four minutes.

Sprinkle the *chaat masala* and lemon juice and serve hot with Green Chutney (page 94).

Sichuan Vegetable Fingers

1 medium carrot, grated
¼ medium cauliflower, grated
1 small green capsicum, finely chopped
¼ small cabbage, finely chopped
8-10 French beans, finely chopped
1 small onion, finely chopped
Salt to taste
5 tablespoons cornflour
2 tablespoons refined four
2 teaspoons red chilli flakes
¼ teaspoon MSG (optional)
2 tablespoons finely chopped fresh coriander
¼ teaspoon white pepper powder
1 teaspoon light soy sauce
1 tablespoon oil + for deep-frying

In a large bowl, combine the carrot, cauliflower, capsicum, cabbage, French beans, onion and salt. Set aside for ten to fifteen minutes. Squeeze the vegetables to remove excess water.

Add three tablespoons of cornflour, the flour, chilli flakes, MSG, fresh coriander, white pepper powder and soy sauce to the vegetables, and mix well. Divide the mixture into sixteen equal portions and roll into balls. Shape each ball into two-inch long fingers. Dust the vegetable fingers with two tablespoons of cornflour.

Heat plenty of oil in a non-stick wok and deep-fry the vegetable fingers till golden brown and crisp. Drain on absorbent paper. Serve hot with Sichuan Sauce (page 95).

Sichuan Vegetable Fingers

Mini Tostadas

Mini Tostadas

12 ready-made corn tostadas

A few iceberg lettuce leaves, torn into bite-sized pieces

1 tablespoon pomegranate kernels

A few sprigs of fresh parsley

Salsa

½ cup sweetcorn kernels

1 tablespoon olive oil

1 medium onion, chopped

1 medium green capsicum, cut into small pieces

1 medium red capsicum, cut into small pieces

1 medium yellow capsicum, cut into small pieces

50 grams cottage cheese, cut into small pieces

7-8 black peppercorns, crushed

¼ teaspoon paprika

1 tablespoon chopped fresh coriander

Salt to taste

1 tablespoon lemon juice

1 tablespoon balsamic vinegar (optional)

For the salsa, roast the corn in a non-stick pan over high heat to scorch the kernels lightly. Add the olive oil and onion, and sauté till translucent. Remove from heat and transfer to a bowl. Set aside to cool.

Place the capsicums and cottage cheese in a separate bowl. Add the crushed peppercorns, paprika, chopped coriander, salt and lemon juice, and mix well.

Add the sautéed corn and balsamic vinegar. Adjust salt and toss to mix.

To assemble, place the tostadas on a plate and place a piece of lettuce leaf on each one. Spoon some salsa on each tostada.

Garnish with pomegranate kernels and parsley sprigs, and serve immediately.

Chef's Tip: Ready-made tostadas are available in most grocery stores or supermarkets.

Golden Bags

30 five-inch round spring roll wrappers
1 cup crumbled cottage cheese
½ cup minced mixed vegetables (cauliflower, French beans and green peas)
1 tablespoon chopped fresh coriander
¼ teaspoon black pepper powder
Salt to taste
2 tablespoons oil + for deep-frying
10 garlic cloves, chopped
A few spring onion greens
½ cup sweet chilli sauce

To make the filling, mix together the cottage cheese, vegetables, chopped coriander, pepper powder and salt.

Heat two tablespoons of oil in a non-stick wok; add the garlic and sauté until fragrant. Add the cottage cheese mixture and stir-fry for three to four minutes.

Place one tablespoon of the filling in the centre of each spring roll wrapper, and gather the edges together in pleats to make a bag (*potli*). Tie the bag tightly around the filling with a strip of spring onion green stalk. Trim the excess wrapper and spring onion.

Heat plenty of oil in a deep non-stick wok and deep-fry the bags until golden. Drain on absorbent paper. Serve hot with sweet chilli sauce.

Potli Kabab

4 (115 grams each) boneless chicken breasts
250 grams minced chicken
2 tablespoons ginger-garlic paste
2 tablespoons chopped fresh coriander
5-8 fresh mint leaves, chopped
2 green chillies, chopped
Salt to taste

½ cup drained yogurt
2 tablespoons gram flour
2 tablespoons cream
1 teaspoon green chilli paste
½ teaspoon *garam masala* powder
Melted butter for basting

Slit the chicken breasts without cutting through. Open them out. Flatten slightly with a steak hammer or with the back of a knife.

Marinate the minced chicken in a mixture of one tablespoon ginger-garlic paste, chopped coriander, fresh mint, green chillies and salt for about fifteen minutes.

Divide the chicken mixture into four equal portions and shape them into balls. Place each ball on a flattened chicken breast. Shape the chicken breast around the ball to cover it completely. Seal the edges with a toothpick.

Place the yogurt in a bowl; add the gram flour, remaining ginger-garlic paste, salt, cream, green chilli paste and *garam masala* powder and mix well.

Marinate the stuffed chicken balls in this mixture for two hours preferably in a refrigerator.

Preheat the oven to 200°C/400°F/Gas Mark 6.

Place the balls sealed end facing down on a greased baking tray keeping a distance of an inch between each ball.

Cook in the preheated oven for twenty minutes basting with the melted butter a few times in between.

Transfer to a plate. Serve hot with a salad and chutney of your choice.

Chef's Tip: If the minced chicken is not very fine, grind a couple of times in a blender.

Paneer Ke Tinke

- 300 grams cottage cheese, cut into 1-inch cubes
- 1 teaspoon oil + for shallow-frying
- 2 tablespoons gram flour
- ¾ cup drained (hung) yogurt
- 1 teaspoon roasted cumin powder
- 3-4 black peppercorns, crushed
- ½ teaspoon roasted crushed dried fenugreek leaves
- ½ teaspoon turmeric powder
- ½ teaspoon *garam masala* powder
- 5 teaspoons lemon juice
- Salt to taste
- A few saffron threads (optional)
- 1 medium onion, cut into 1-inch pieces, layers separated
- 1 medium green capsicum, cut into 1-inch pieces
- 1 medium red capsicum, cut into 1-inch pieces
- 6 satay sticks

Heat one teaspoon of oil in a non-stick pan and roast the gram flour on low heat till fragrant. Place the yogurt, cumin powder, peppercorns, dried fenugreek leaves, turmeric powder, *garam masala* powder, lemon juice, salt and saffron in a bowl and mix well. Add the roasted gram flour and mix well. Add the cottage cheese cubes and toss gently. Set aside to marinate for ten to fifteen minutes.

Thread the ingredients in the following order onto the satay sticks: onion, cottage cheese, green capsicum, red capsicum, cottage cheese, onion. Heat a shallow non-stick pan; add the remaining oil and place the satay sticks on it.

Cook on medium heat, turning the satay sticks from time to time so that the cottage cheese pieces are cooked evenly all around. Serve hot with Mint Chutney (page 94).

Tandoori Subz Shaslik

200 grams pineapple, cut into 1½-inch cubes
2 medium green capsicums, cut into 1½-inch pieces
2 medium onions, cut into 1½-inch pieces
2 medium tomatoes, seeded and cut into 1½-inch pieces
Salt to taste
2 teaspoons red chilli powder
1½ teaspoons powdered dried fenugreek leaves
2 teaspoons *garam masala* powder
1 teaspoon *chaat masala*
2 tablespoons vinegar
1 tablespoon oil

In a bowl, mix together the salt, chilli powder, powdered dried fenugreek leaves, *garam masala* powder, *chaat masala*, vinegar and oil. Add the pineapple and vegetables and mix thoroughly. Set aside to marinade for one hour.

Thread the pineapple, capsicum, onion and tomato one after the other onto toothpicks. Pour the remaining marinade on top.

Heat a non-stick *tawa*, place the toothpicks on it and cook over a medium heat, turning the toothpicks a few times so that the vegetables cook evenly on all sides. Cook till lightly coloured. Serve hot with a salad and chutney of your choice.

Salt And Pepper Prawns

300 grams king prawns
Salt to taste
½ teaspoon black pepper powder
4 black peppercorns, crushed
2 tablespoons cornflour
2 tablespoons light soy sauce
1½ tablespoons oil + for deep-frying
3 garlic cloves, crushed
¾ inch ginger, chopped
2 spring onions, sliced
3 spring onion greens stalks, sliced

Peel the prawns leaving the tails intact; devein and wash thoroughly.

In a bowl, combine the salt, one-fourth teaspoon pepper powder, half the crushed peppercorns, one tablespoon of cornflour and one tablespoon of soy sauce.

Add the prawns, mix well and set aside to marinate for fifteen minutes. Mix the remaining cornflour with two tablespoons of water.

Heat sufficient oil in a non-stick wok and deep-fry the prawns for two minutes. Drain on absorbent paper.

In a separate non-stick wok, heat one and a half tablespoons of oil; add the garlic, ginger and spring onions, and sauté for two minutes on high heat.

Add the prawns, salt, remaining pepper powder, half the remaining crushed peppercorns, remaining soy sauce, the cornflour mixture and spring onion greens. Stir-fry on high heat for four minutes, or until the prawns are cooked through.

Sprinkle the remaining crushed peppercorns and serve hot.

Chicken 65

450 grams boneless chicken, cut into 1½-inch pieces
½ cup yogurt
1½ tablespoons lemon juice
2 tablespoons rice flour
Salt to taste
6 tablespoons oil

Masala

4 dried red chillies
2 inches ginger
6 garlic cloves
2 tablespoons coriander seeds
12-15 black peppercorns

Grind the ingredients of the *masala* to a fine paste.

Mix the yogurt, lemon juice, rice flour, salt and two tablespoons oil into the ground *masala* paste.

Coat the chicken with the *masala* paste and marinate for an hour in a refrigerator.

Heat the remaining oil in a thick-bottomed non-stick *kadai*; add the chicken pieces in small batches of six to eight pieces and stir-fry over high heat for one minute, tossing continuously. Add another batch of the chicken and repeat.

Lower heat once all the chicken has been added. Turn the pieces frequently, basting with the remaining *masala*.

Cook till the oil separates and the chicken turns crispy on the outside, but moist and soft on the inside.

Adjust salt, toss well and remove. Drain and serve hot.

Fish Tikka Achaari

- 2 (400 grams), king fish fillets, cut into 2-inch pieces
- 2 tablespoons lemon juice
- Salt to taste
- 1 teaspoon garlic paste
- 1 teaspoon ginger paste
- ½ teaspoon turmeric powder
- 2 teaspoons Kashmiri chilli powder
- 1 teaspoon mustard seeds, roasted
- 1 teaspoon fennel seeds
- 1 teaspoon onion seeds
- ½ teaspoon fenugreek seeds
- ½ teaspoon black salt
- 2 tablespoons mustard oil
- 1 cup yogurt, whisked
- 4 tablespoons butter, melted

Place the fish fillets in a bowl; add the lemon juice, salt, garlic paste, ginger paste, turmeric powder and chilli powder, and mix well.

Heat a non-stick pan and dry-roast the mustard seeds, fennel seeds, onion seeds and fenugreek seeds. Crush them along with the black salt with a mortar and pestle.

Add the yogurt along with the crushed spices to the fish mixture and mix. Leave to stand for thirty minutes.

Heat the mustard oil in a non-stick pan to smoking point. Set aside to cool.

Preheat an oven to 220°C/425°F/Gas Mark 7.

Add the cooled mustard oil to the marinated fish and mix.

Place the fish on a greased rack over a tray in the preheated oven. Cook, for ten to fifteen minutes or till tender, basting with butter once while cooking.

Serve hot.

Chef's Tip: If you do not have an oven, you can thread the pieces of fish onto a skewer and cook them on a hot non-stick *tawa*.

Baked Mixed Vegetables

3 medium brinjals, sliced
4 medium potatoes, boiled and sliced
1 medium green capsicum, sliced
1 medium red capsicum, sliced
2 medium onions, cut into round slices, rings separated
Salt to taste
2 tablespoons oil
¼ cup Vegetable Stock (page 95)
10-12 black peppercorns, crushed
½ cup fresh breadcrumbs
½ cup grated processed cheese

Tomato Sauce

1 cup Tomato Concassé (see Note)
2 tablespoons oil
3-4 garlic cloves, chopped
4-5 black peppercorns
1 bay leaf
Salt to taste

Cheese Sauce

½ cup White Sauce (page 95)
¼ cup grated processed cheese

Preheat an oven to 200°C/400°F/Gas Mark 6.

Sprinkle salt on the brinjal slices. Place in a colander for thirty minutes to drain. Rinse under cold running water and pat dry with paper towels.

Arrange the brinjal slices on a baking tray and grill in the preheated oven till golden brown.

Heat the oil in a non-stick pan. Add the onion rings and sauté for a minute. Add the green and red capsicums and sauté for one or two minutes. Set aside.

For the tomato sauce, heat the oil in a pan. Add the garlic and sauté for one minute. Add the tomato concassé and sauté for two or three minutes.

Add the peppercorns, bay leaf and salt and continue to cook for two or three minutes, or till the sauce thickens.

To make the cheese sauce, add the grated cheese to the white sauce and mix well.

Add the cheese sauce to the tomato sauce; add one-fourth cup of vegetable stock and bring the mixture to a boil. Remove from heat and strain.

In a seven-inch square baking dish, layer the onions, green and red capsicums followed by the brinjals and potatoes. Sprinkle salt and crushed peppercorns over each layer.

Pour the tomato-cheese sauce over all the vegetables.

Sprinkle the fresh breadcrumbs and top with the grated cheese. Bake for about twenty minutes, or till the cheese turns golden.

Serve hot with brown bread.

Note: To make 1 cup of tomato concassé, blanch 5 medium tomatoes in plenty of boiling water for two minutes. Drain and refresh in cold water; peel, cut in half, remove the seeds and chop roughly.

Baked Mixed Vegetables

Chole Dhania Masala

Chole Dhania Masala

- ¾ cup chickpeas
- 1½ teaspoons coriander seeds
- 1 small bunch (50 grams) fresh coriander
- ¼ cup split Bengal gram
- Salt to taste
- ½ inch cinnamon
- 1½ teaspoons cumin seeds
- 1 black cardamom
- 4-5 cloves
- 2 green chillies
- 4 tablespoons ghee
- 1 medium onion, sliced
- 1 teaspoon garlic paste
- 1 teaspoon ginger paste
- ½ tablespoon dried mango powder
- ½ teaspoon *garam masala* powder
- Black salt to taste
- ¼ teaspoon red chilli powder

Soak the chickpeas and split Bengal gram separately for four to six hours. Drain, mix, add three cups of water and a little salt, and pressure-cook till the pressure is released five to six times (five to six whistles).

Lightly roast and powder the cinnamon, cumin seeds, coriander seeds, black cardamom and cloves. Grind together the fresh coriander and green chillies to a smooth paste.

Heat three tablespoons ghee in a non-stick *kadai*; add the onion and sauté for three to four minutes till golden brown. Add the garlic paste and ginger paste, and continue to sauté for another minute.

Add the spice powder, dried mango powder, *garam masala* powder, black salt and coriander paste, and sauté for two to three minutes or till the ghee separates from the *masala.*

Add the chickpeas and split Bengal gram, and mix. Add half a cup of water if the mixture is too dry. Adjust the salt and let the mixture come to a boil. Lower the heat and simmer for four to five minutes.

Heat the remaining ghee in a small non-stick pan; take it off the heat and add the chilli powder and immediately pour over the *chole.* Cover immediately and leave to stand for five minutes.

Serve hot with *roti* or *puri.*

Handi Biryani

1½ cups rice, soaked and drained
4 medium onions
A few saffron threads
A few drops *kewra* water
Salt to taste
2-3 green cardamoms
1 black cardamom
2-3 cloves
1 inch cinnamon
1 bay leaf
1 medium carrot, cut into ½-inch cubes
¼ medium cauliflower, cut into small florets
10-15 French beans, cut into ½-inch pieces
½ cup green peas
2 tablespoons oil + for deep-frying
½ teaspoon caraway seeds
½ tablespoon ginger paste
½ tablespoon garlic paste
4-5 green chillies, chopped
1 tablespoon coriander powder
1 teaspoon turmeric powder
1 teaspoon red chilli powder
¾ cup yogurt
2 medium tomatoes, chopped
½ teaspoon *garam masala* powder
2 tablespoons chopped fresh coriander
2 tablespoons chopped fresh mint leaves
2 tablespoons ghee
1 inch ginger, cut into thin strips

Chop one onion and slice the others. Soak the saffron in *kewra* water.

Cook the rice in four cups of boiling salted water with green cardamoms, black cardamom, cloves, cinnamon and bay leaf, until three-fourth done. Drain and set aside.

Mix together the carrot, cauliflower, French beans and peas and boil in three cups of salted water till three-fourth done. Drain and refresh under cold running water. Set aside. Heat plenty of oil in a non-stick *kadai* and deep-fry the sliced onions till golden brown. Drain on absorbent paper and set aside.

Heat two tablespoons of oil in a thick-bottomed non-stick pan and add the caraway seeds. When they begin to change colour, add the chopped onion and sauté until golden brown. Add the ginger paste, garlic paste and green chillies and stir. Add the coriander powder, turmeric powder, chilli powder and yogurt and mix well. Add the tomatoes and cook on medium heat till the oil separates. Add the boiled vegetables and salt and mix well.

In a *handi*, arrange alternate layers of cooked vegetables and rice. Sprinkle the saffron-flavoured *kewra* water, *garam masala* powder, chopped coriander, mint leaves, fried onions and ghee in between the layers and on top. Make sure that you end with the rice layer topped with saffron and spices.

Cover and seal with aluminum foil or *roti* dough. Place the *handi* on a *tawa* and cook on low heat for twenty minutes. Garnish with ginger strips and serve hot with a *raita*.

Paneer Kaliya

500 grams cottage cheese, cut into 1-inch cubes
½ cup almonds, blanched, peeled and ground
2 tablespoons pure ghee
4 green cardamoms
4 cloves
10 black peppercorns
1 inch cinnamon
2 medium onions, sliced
1 inch ginger, chopped
2 tablespoons coriander seeds
½ teaspoon turmeric powder
Salt to taste
2 tablespoons chopped fresh coriander

Heat one tablespoon of ghee in a non-stick *kadai*. Crush the cardamoms, cloves and peppercorns with a mortar and pestle and add to the ghee. Add the cinnamon and onions and sauté for two to three minutes.

Add the ginger and coriander seeds and sauté for a minute longer. Remove from the heat, cool slightly and grind into a fine paste with one tablespoon water.

Heat the remaining ghee in a non-stick pan, add the ground *masala* paste and sauté until ghee separates. Add one tablespoon of water to prevent scorching.

Mix the almond paste with one cup of water and add to the *masala*. Add the turmeric powder and simmer for a while. Add salt to taste and mix well.

Add the cottage cheese cubes and simmer for ten minutes. Serve hot garnished with the chopped coriander.

Potato Cheese Balls In Spinach Gravy

2 medium potatoes, boiled and mashed
200 grams cottage cheese, mashed
3 tablespoons cornflour
½ teaspoon red chilli powder
½ inch ginger, chopped
Salt to taste
½ teaspoon white pepper powder
12-15 cashew nuts, chopped
12-15 raisins
Oil for deep-frying

Spinach Gravy

500 grams fresh spinach leaves
2 green chillies, chopped
3 tablespoons oil
½ teaspoon caraway seeds
5-6 garlic cloves, chopped
½ cup tomato purée
½ teaspoon turmeric powder
1 teaspoon coriander powder
Salt to taste
1 teaspoon *garam masala* powder
¼ cup cream

Mix together the mashed cottage cheese and potatoes, cornflour, chilli powder, ginger, salt and white pepper powder. Divide the mixture into sixteen balls. Stuff each ball with cashew nuts and raisins.

Heat plenty of oil in a non-stick *kadai* and deep-fry the balls, a few at a time, until golden brown. Drain on absorbent paper and set aside.

For the gravy, blanch the spinach in plenty of water; refresh under cold running water and drain well. Blend with the green chillies to a smooth purée.

Heat three tablespoons of oil in a non-stick *handi*; add the caraway seeds and garlic and stir-fry for a few minutes. Add the spinach purée and cook for about two to three minutes. Stir in the tomato purée and mix well.

Add the turmeric powder, coriander powder and salt. Stir and cook for four to five minutes.

Add one cup of water and bring to a boil. Lower heat and simmer for five to seven minutes. Stir in the *garam masala* powder and cook till the curry is reduced by half. Lower heat, stir in the cream and cook for half a minute. Remove from heat.

Arrange the *kofte* in a serving dish. Pour the hot gravy over and serve hot.

Potato Cheese Balls in Spinach Gravy

Penne with Creamy Pesto and Cherry Tomatoes

Penne With Creamy Pesto And Cherry Tomatoes

200 grams penne pasta (quill-shaped pasta), cooked
¼ cup cream
20 cherry tomatoes
2 tablespoons olive oil
2 garlic cloves, sliced
5-6 black peppercorns, crushed
Salt to taste

Pesto Sauce

30-40 (¾ cup) basil leaves
4 garlic cloves
3 tablespoons pine nuts
¼ cup crumbled Parmesan cheese
5 tablespoons olive oil

For the pesto sauce, grind together the basil leaves, garlic, pine nuts and Parmesan cheese. Add the olive oil little by little and grind till smooth.

Heat two tablespoons olive oil in a non-stick pan.

Add the sliced garlic and sauté till golden. Add the cherry tomatoes, pasta, peppercorns and salt and toss to mix.

Add the pesto sauce and toss. Add the cream and toss again till the pasta is coated with the sauce. Cook for a minute till heated through. Serve hot.

Seafood Pad Thai

12 small prawns, peeled and deveined

100 grams fish fillets, cut into 1-inch pieces

8-10 mussels or clams

200 grams flat noodles, boiled

3 tablespoons oil

5-6 spring onions, chopped

5-6 garlic cloves, chopped

1 medium green capsicum, cut into thin strips

Salt to taste

1 teaspoon soy sauce

2 tablespoons brown sugar

2 fresh red chillies, diagonally sliced

5-6 spring onion green stalks, chopped

3 tablespoons roasted peanuts, coarsely ground

1 tablespoon lemon juice

½ cup bean sprouts

Pat the prawns dry with a kitchen towel. Open the mussels or clam shells with a knife and scoop out the meat.

Heat the oil in a non-stick pan; add the spring onions, garlic, prawns, fish and mussels or clams and green capsicum, and toss to mix.

Add the noodles, salt, soy sauce, brown sugar, and toss some more.

Add the red chillies, spring onion greens and most of the roasted peanuts one after the other, tossing after each addition.

Transfer to a serving dish. Sprinkle the lemon juice and bean sprouts, and top with the remaining roasted peanuts. Serve at once.

Note: To cook the noodles, bring seven to eight cups of water to a boil in a large non-stick pan. Add the flat noodles and cook till *al dente* (cooked, but still firm to the bite). Drain and refresh in cold water. Spread on a plate to cool.

Chops Do Pyaza

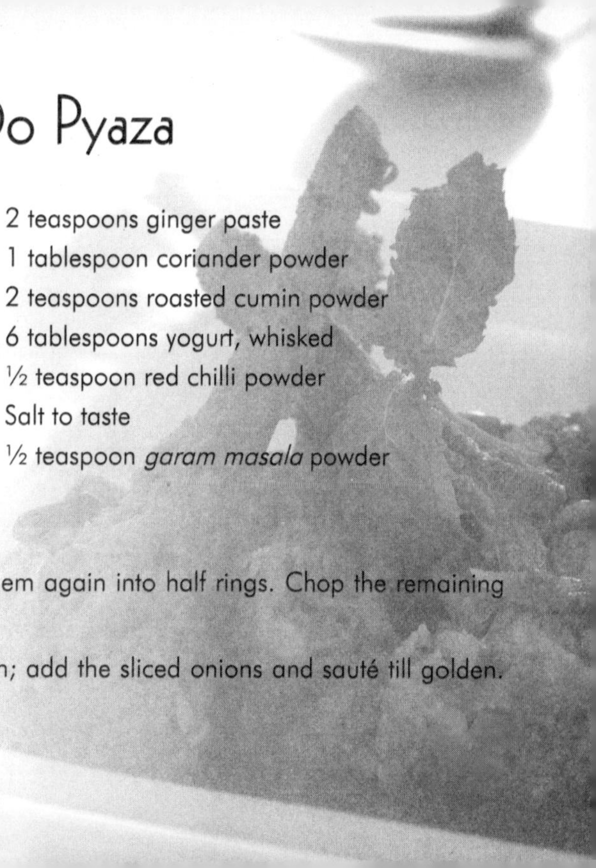

- 1 kilogram lamb chops
- 4 large onions
- 10 tablespoons oil
- 1 inch cinnamon
- 10 green cardamoms
- 10 cloves
- 2 teaspoons garlic paste
- 2 teaspoons ginger paste
- 1 tablespoon coriander powder
- 2 teaspoons roasted cumin powder
- 6 tablespoons yogurt, whisked
- ½ teaspoon red chilli powder
- Salt to taste
- ½ teaspoon *garam masala* powder

Cut three onions in half vertically and slice them again into half rings. Chop the remaining onion.

Heat the oil in a thick-bottomed non-stick pan; add the sliced onions and sauté till golden. Drain on absorbent paper.

Add the cinnamon, cardamoms and cloves to the oil remaining in the pan and stir-fry over medium heat till fragrant. Add the lamb chops, a few at a time and stir-fry till brown. Drain and place them in a bowl.

Add the chopped onion to the same pan and sauté till golden brown. Add the garlic and ginger pastes and sauté over medium heat till the oil separates. Add the coriander powder and cumin powder and continue to sauté for half a minute.

Add the yogurt, one tablespoon at a time, and sauté till incorporated into the *masala*. Add the lamb chops, one and a half cups of water, chilli powder and salt. Mix well and bring the mixture to a boil.

Cover, lower heat and cook for about forty-five minutes until the lamb is tender. If the dish is too dry, add half a cup of warm water.

Add the fried onions and *garam masala* powder and mix well. Adjust seasoning and continue to cook, uncovered, for another two to three minutes, stirring gently. Serve hot.

Iggaru Royya

Coastal Kerala Prawn Curry

- 36 (350 grams) medium prawns
- 5 tablespoons oil
- 1 cup grated fresh coconut
- 8 dried red chillies, broken
- 1 teaspoon cumin seeds
- ½ teaspoon fenugreek seeds
- 10-12 black peppercorns
- 2 medium onions, chopped
- 2 teaspoons ginger paste
- 2 teaspoons garlic paste
- 2 medium tomatoes, chopped
- Salt to taste
- 10-12 curry leaves
- 2 tablespoons chopped fresh coriander

Peel and devein the prawns and pat them dry.

Heat two tablespoons of oil in a non-stick *kadai* and sauté the coconut with dried chillies, cumin seeds, fenugreek seeds and black peppercorns till the coconut turns light brown. Cool and grind to a coarse paste.

Heat the remaining oil in the same *kadai*; add the onions and sauté till golden brown. Add the ginger paste, garlic paste and sauté till all the moisture evaporates. Add the ground paste and stir.

Add the tomatoes, salt, curry leaves and sauté on low heat for three to four minutes. Add the prawns, toss well and cook till the prawns are done.

Garnish with the chopped coriander and serve hot.

Chef's Tip: Traditionally it should be a thick *masala*, but if you want to serve it with rice make the curry a little thinner.

Iggaru Royya

Green Chilli Chicken

Green Chilli Chicken

- 1 whole (800 grams) chicken, cut into 1½-inch pieces
- 1 cup whole small green chillies
- 3 green chillies, chopped
- 2 medium onions, quartered
- 10 garlic cloves
- 1½ inches ginger, sliced
- ½ cup chopped fresh coriander
- Salt to taste
- 3 tablespoons oil
- ¾ teaspoon cumin seeds
- ¼ teaspoon turmeric powder
- 1 teaspoon roasted cumin powder
- 2 teaspoons coriander powder
- 1 teaspoon *garam masala* powder

Grind together the chopped green chillies, onions, garlic, ginger, chopped coriander and salt.

Marinate the chicken in this mixture for about half an hour.

Heat the oil in a non-stick *kadai* and add the cumin seeds. When they begin to change colour, add the turmeric powder.

Add the marinated chicken and the whole small green chillies, and mix well. Add the cumin powder and coriander powder, and stir to mix.

Add the *garam masala* powder and adjust the seasoning. Stir in half a cup of water, cover and cook over medium heat for eight to ten minutes.

Lower the heat and cook for another eight to ten minutes, or till the chicken is tender.

Serve hot.

Mughlai Gosht Biryani

750 grams mutton on the bone, cut into 1-inch pieces
1½ cups Basmati rice, cooked
Salt to taste
1 medium onion, chopped
4 garlic cloves
1 inch ginger, coarsely chopped
15-20 almonds, blanched and slivered
A generous pinch of saffron threads
1 tablespoon milk
½ cup oil
1 cup yogurt
¼ teaspoon red chilli powder
2 tablespoons butter
1 cup deep-fried onions
3 hard-boiled eggs, quartered
10-12 sultanas, fried

Masala Powder

5-6 cloves
5-6 bluck peppercorns
½ teaspoon green cardamom seeds
1 teaspoon cumin seeds
1 teaspoon coriander seeds
1 inch cinnamon
¼ teaspoon grated nutmeg

Grind the onion, garlic, ginger and half the almonds with three tablespoons of water into a smooth paste. Soak the saffron in the milk.

Heat the oil in a thick-bottomed non-stick frying pan; add the remaining almonds and fry till golden. Drain. In the same pan, fry the mutton, a few pieces at a time, till brown. Drain.

In the remaining oil, sauté the onion-almond paste till medium brown. Add the fried mutton, stir well and add the yogurt and salt. Stir in one cup of water and cook, covered, over low heat for thirty minutes.

Grind together all the ingredients for the *masala* powder. Add to the mutton with the chilli powder. Continue to cook for thirty minutes, or till the mutton is tender and the gravy is thick and smooth.

Preheat the oven to 150°C/300°F/Gas Mark 2.

Grease a large baking dish with the butter. Pour the mutton with its gravy into the dish. Cover with the rice and sprinkle with saffron and half the browned onions. Cover with foil and cook in the oven for one hour.

Just before serving, mix the contents lightly and garnish with boiled eggs, remaining browned onions, fried sultanas and almonds.

Chilli-Lemon Stewed Vegetables With Noodles

2 green chillies, sliced
2 lemon grass stalks, chopped
1 tablespoon lemon juice
7-8 cauliflower florets, finely sliced
7-8 fresh button mushrooms, finely sliced
¼ cup sweetcorn kernels
1 small green capsicum, cut into ½-inch pieces
½ medium red capsicum, cut into ½-inch pieces
½ medium yellow capsicum, cut into ½-inch pieces
¼ cup bean sprouts
2 medium tomatoes, cut into 1-inch pieces
¼ cup boiled noodles
3 tablespoons oil
4 cups Vegetable Stock (page 95)
1 teaspoon cornflour
Salt to taste
5-6 black peppercorns, crushed

Heat one tablespoon of oil in a non-stick wok. Add the noodles and sauté till light brown. Transfer to a serving dish and keep warm.

Heat the remaining oil in the same wok. Add the green chillies and lemon grass and sauté for a minute. Add the cauliflower, mushrooms, corn, capsicums, bean sprouts and tomatoes and stir-fry for a few minutes.

Stir in the vegetable stock and bring the mixture to a boil. Add the cornflour mixed in one tablespoon of water and stir. Cook till the mixture thickens slightly.

Add the salt, crushed peppercorns and lemon juice and mix gently. Pour over the noodles and serve hot.

Jammu Ka Aloo-Anardana Parantha

- 2 large potatoes, boiled and mashed
- 1 teaspoon pomegranate seeds, roasted and powdered
- 2 cups wholewheat flour
- Salt to taste
- 2 tablespoons milk
- 2 tablespoons yogurt
- 1 small onion, chopped
- ½ teaspoon red chilli powder
- 2 green chillies, chopped
- 1 teaspoon *chaat masala*
- 2 tablespoons chopped fresh coriander

Place the flour in a bowl; add the salt, milk, yogurt and sufficient water and knead into a soft dough. Cover with a damp cloth and set aside for fifteen minutes. Divide the dough into eight portions.

Add the onion to the mashed potatoes along with the chilli powder, green chillies, roasted pomegranate seeds powder, *chaat masala*, chopped coriander and salt and mix well. Divide into eight portions.

Roll out each portion of the dough into a small *puri*; place one portion of potato stuffing in the centre, gather in the edges and roll into a ball. Roll out into a *parantha*.

Heat a *tawa*. Place a *parantha* on it and roast for half a minute. Flip over and moisten the top lightly with a little water. Flip over again and moisten the other side as well. Continue to cook till both sides are evenly browned. Serve hot with fresh yogurt.

Herb And Garlic Bread

- 1 tablespoon dried oregano
- 10-12 garlic cloves, chopped
- 1 French loaf
- 100 grams butter

Preheat oven to 200°C/400°F/Gas Mark 6.

Soften the butter, add the oregano and garlic and mix well.

Cut the loaf into one-inch thick slices without cutting through. Spread the garlic butter between the slices. Wrap the loaf in aluminium foil and bake in the preheated oven for fifteen minutes.

Separate the slices and serve warm.

Herb and Garlic Bread

Grapes and Walnut Raita

Grapes And Walnut Raita

- 25-30 green grapes, halved
- ¼ cup walnut kernels, chopped
- 2 cups yogurt, whisked
- Salt to taste
- 1½ teaspoons sugar
- ½ teaspoon roasted cumin powder
- 2 tablespoons chopped fresh mint
- A large pinch red chilli powder

Whisk the yogurt in a large bowl with salt, sugar and cumin powder.

Add grapes, walnuts and mint and fold in gently. Place in refrigerator to chill.

Sprinkle chilli powder and serve.

Methiwali Arhar Dal

- 125 grams fresh fenugreek leaves, chopped
- 1 cup split pigeon peas
- ½ teaspoon turmeric powder
- Salt to taste
- 1 teaspoon grated jaggery
- 1 tablespoon pure ghee
- 6 garlic cloves
- ¼ teaspoon asafoetida
- ½ teaspoon red chilli powder

Soak the split pigeon peas in two cups of water for one hour. Drain.

Pressure-cook the soaked pigeon peas in three cups of water with the turmeric powder till the pressure is released four times (four whistles). Remove the lid when the pressure reduces completely and mash the *dal* well with the back of a ladle. Add half a cup of water and jaggery, and bring to a boil. Cook for a few minutes.

Heat the ghee in a non-stick pan; add the garlic and asafoetida, and sauté till the garlic turns light brown. Add the fenugreek leaves and sauté for two to three minutes. Add the *dal* and chilli powder, and stir well. Adjust the consistency, if necessary, by adding water. Serve hot.

Bhinda Ni Kadhi

- 15 ladies' fingers, cut into ½-inch pieces
- 3 tablespoons oil
- 2 cups sour yogurt
- 4 tablespoons gram flour
- ½ teaspoon turmeric powder
- 1 teaspoon red chilli powder
- Sugar to taste (optional)
- Salt to taste
- ¾ teaspoon mustard seeds
- ½ teaspoon fenugreek seeds
- 1 inch ginger, cut into thin strips
- 2 green chillies, chopped
- ¼ teaspoon asafoetida
- 2 tablespoons chopped fresh coriander

Heat two tablespoons of oil in a non-stick pan; add the ladies' fingers and sauté till lightly browned. Whisk together the yogurt, gram flour, turmeric powder, chilli powder, sugar and salt till smooth. Add four cups of water and whisk again.

Heat the remaining oil in a non-stick *kadai*; add the mustard seeds and fenugreek seeds. When they begin to splutter, add the ginger, green chillies and asafoetida, and sauté for half a minute. Add the yogurt mixture and bring to a boil. Lower heat and cook, stirring continuously, till quite thick.

Add the fried ladies' fingers and simmer for two or three minutes. Garnish with chopped coriander and serve hot.

Tiramisù

12 slices chocolate sponge cake (175 grams each)
½ tablespoon unflavoured gelatine
1 cup thick cream
½ cup powdered sugar
3 egg yolks
¼ cup sugar
2 tablespoons + 2 teaspoons instant coffee powder
¾ cup mascarpone cheese
Chocolate curls, to decorate

Cut each slice of cake in half. Dissolve the gelatine in three tablespoons of hot water. Whip the cream with powdered sugar till stiff and set aside.

Whip the egg yolks with sugar and one tablespoon of water in a double boiler, or in a heatproof bowl over a pan of simmering water, till the mixture forms thick ribbons. Set aside to cool.

Mix two tablespoons of instant coffee powder in half a cup of water and soak the chocolate sponge fingers in this mixture. Arrange half the sponge fingers in a layer at the base of a spring form tin.

Mix two teaspoons of instant coffee powder in one teaspoon of water. Add this along with mascarpone cheese and gelatine to the egg mixture and mix well. Fold in the whipped cream.

Pour half the mixture over the chocolate fingers. Arrange the remaining chocolate fingers over the cheese mixture and top with the remaining mixture and level the top. Place it in the refrigerator till set.

Remove from the tin, cut into wedges and serve chilled, decorated with chocolate curls.

Gil-E-Firdaus

5 tablespoons raw rice
250 grams bottle gourd, grated
2 tablespoons pure ghee
6 cups milk
100 grams *khoya/mawa*, grated
½ cup sugar
A few drops rose essence
10 almonds, sliced
A few rose petals

Soak the rice in a cup of water for about one hour. Drain and spread out to dry and grind coarsely.

Bring one cup of water to a boil in a pan and add the bottle gourd. Cook till soft, drain and set aside.

Heat the ghee in a deep non-stick pan, add the rice and sauté for a few seconds. Add the milk and bring to a boil. Lower heat and cook till the rice is soft. Add the bottle gourd and simmer for five minutes.

Add the *khoya* and sugar and cook till the mixture is thick enough to coat the back of a spoon. Stir in the rose essence. Pour into individual serving bowls and set aside to cool. Sprinkle sliced almonds and rose petals on top and serve chilled.

Quick Chocolate Mousse

300 grams dark chocolate, broken into small pieces
2 tablespoons butter
6 cups double cream
½ cup caster sugar

Place the chocolate and butter in a double-boiler or in a bowl over a pan of hot water.

Cook over medium heat till the chocolate melts and the mixture is smooth. Remove from heat and leave to cool. Stir half the cream into the melted chocolate.

Beat the remaining cream with sugar till stiff; fold gently into the chocolate mixture and refrigerate for thirty minutes.

Spoon the chilled chocolate mousse into a piping bag fitted with a large star nozzle and pipe the mousse into individual glasses.

Refrigerate and serve chilled.

Badam-Pista Kulfi

- 12-15 almonds, coarsely ground
- 15-20 pistachios, coarsely ground
- 1½ litres milk
- A pinch of saffron
- 1 tin (400 grams) sweetened condensed milk
- ¼ cup *khoya/mawa*, grated

Heat the milk in a thick-bottomed non-stick pan. When the milk begins to boil, add the saffron, lower the heat and simmer, stirring continuously, till the milk is reduced by half.

Add the condensed milk, almonds and pistachios, and mix well. Cook for three to four minutes, stirring continuously. Take the pan off the heat and set aside to let cool. Add the *khoya* and mix well.

Pour into individual *kulfi* moulds and place them in the freezer to set. Unmould and serve immediately.

Note: Keep a jar of equal amounts of ground almonds, pistachios and cardamom handy, which can be added to *kulfi* and other desserts.

Badam-Pista Kulfi

Kesari Phirni

Kesari Phirni

A few saffron threads
2 cups milk
3 tablespoons rice, soaked
3-4 pistachios
½ cup sugar
¼ teaspoon green cardamom powder

Soak the saffron in one tablespoon of milk. Blanch the pistachios, peel and cut into slivers.

Boil the milk in a non-stick pan and set aside. Drain and grind the rice coarsely.

Add the coarsely ground rice to the milk and cook, stirring continuously, to prevent lumps from forming. Add the sugar and mix. Add the cardamom powder and saffron-flavoured milk, and mix. When the mixture starts thickening take it off the heat.

Pour into *kasore* (earthenware bowls) that have been soaked in water for some time. Garnish with the pistachio slivers and place in the refrigerator to chill. Served chilled.

Chef's Tip: You can use brown rice instead of white rice – it will make the *phirni* more nutritious.

Eggless Pineapple Mousse

6 tinned pineapple slices, at room temperature

A few drops pineapple essence

2 teaspoons gelatine

½ tin (200 grams) sweetened condensed milk

3 teaspoons lemon juice

250 grams cream

A few drops of edible yellow colour

1 tablespoon powdered sugar

Glace cherries, as required

Mix gelatine with half cup water in a small non-stick pan. Heat on low heat, stirring continuously, till it dissolves. Pour the condensed milk in a bowl and beat till light and creamy. In another bowl, mix lemon juice with half a cup of pineapple syrup from the tin.

Chop five slices of pineapple. Add the lemon-flavoured pineapple syrup and chopped pineapple to the condensed milk. Pour the gelatine solution into the condensed milk mixture stirring continuously. Freeze the mixture for half an hour till it is thick.

Remove from freezer and beat till smooth. Add two hundred grams of cream and set remaining cream aside for decoration.

Add pineapple essence and yellow colour and beat well. Place it back in the freezer for fifteen to twenty minutes.

Remove from freezer and beat again till smooth. Pour into a serving dish and freeze for one hour or till set. Whip the remaining cream with powdered sugar. Remove the mousse from the freezer. Put the whipped cream in a piping bag fitted with a star nozzle and form rosettes on the surface of the mousse. Place a glace cherry on each rosette and serve immediately.

Shahi Tukre

- 6 white bread slices
- 2 tablespoons olive oil
- 2 cups milk
- 4 tablespoons sugar
- 3-4 saffron threads, crushed
- 1 cup crumbled *khoya/mawa*
- ½ teaspoon green cardamom powder
- 15 cashew nuts, chopped
- 1 tablespoon cudpah nuts
- A few drops rose essence
- 8-10 almonds, chopped
- 1 sheet edible silver foil
- A few rose petals

Preheat an oven to 180°C/350°F/Gas Mark 4.

Remove the crust from bread slices and cut each slice diagonally into two. Brush olive oil on the bread slices and bake in the preheated oven for twenty minutes till golden and crisp. Set aside.

Heat the milk with sugar and saffron. Continue to simmer for twelve to fifteen minutes or till it is reduced to three-fourth its original volume.

Add the crumbled *khoya*, cardamom powder and half the cashew nuts and half the cudpahnuts. Remove from heat and set aside to cool. Add the rose essence.

Arrange the bread slices in a baking dish. Spoon the thickened milk on them. Sprinkle the almonds, remaining cashew nuts and cudpah nuts and bake for further fifteen minutes.

Decorate with rose petals and edible silver foil and serve warm or cold.

Mango Bhapa Doi With Citrus Fruits

½ cup mango pulp
1 cup thick yogurt, whisked
1 tin (400 grams) condensed milk
½ cup milk
A few peeled segments of orange
A few peeled segments of sweet lime
A few pomegranate kernels
A small sprig of fresh mint leaves

Place the condensed milk in a bowl. Add the yogurt, mango pulp and milk and mix well. Transfer the mixture into a steamer container.

Heat sufficient water in a steamer. Cover the container with aluminium foil and place in the steamer.

Cover the steamer and steam for twenty to twenty-five minutes. Cool and place in the refrigerator.

Unmould onto a serving plate. Arrange the orange and sweet lime segments in a decorative pattern all around. Top with a few pomegranate kernels. Place a small sprig of mint leaves on top and serve chilled.

Basic Recipes

Coconut Milk
Process 1 cup grated fresh coconut in a blender with ¼ cup warm water. Pass the ground coconut through a piece of muslin or strainer pressing firmly to extract all the juice, or first milk. Add ¼ cup of warm water to the strained coconut to get the second, thinner milk from the same solids.

Green Chutney
Grind together 1 cup fresh coriander, ½ cup fresh mint, 2-3 green chillies, black salt to taste, ¼ teaspoon sugar and 1 tablespoon lemon juice to a smooth paste using a little water if required.

Mayonnaise
Place 1 egg yolk, salt to taste, ¼ teaspoon each white pepper powder, French mustard and sugar and 1 teaspoon vinegar in a clean bowl and mix thoroughly with a whisk. Alternatively, process the mixture in a blender. Add 1 cup of oil, a little at a time, whisking or blending continuously, until all the oil is incorporated. Add 1 teaspoon lemon juice and adjust seasoning. Store in an airtight jar in a refrigerator.

Mint Chutney
Grind 5 cups mint leaves, 3 cups coriander leaves, 10 green chillies, 3 onions, and 3 inches ginger to a fine paste, adding a little water if required. Stir in 1 tablespoon lemon juice, salt and pomegranate seed powder to taste.

Sichuan Sauce

Boil 10-12 dried red chillies in 1 cup of water for 5 to 7 minutes. Drain, cool and grind to a fine paste. Heat ½ cup oil in a pan; add 10 finely chopped garlic cloves, 2 finely chopped green chillies, 2 finely chopped spring onions and 1 inch ginger, grated, and sauté for 1 minute. Add the red chilli paste and sauté for a few more seconds. Add 2-3 inches celery stalk, finely chopped, 3 tablespoons tomato ketchup and salt to taste, and stir well to mix. Stir in 2 teaspoons white vinegar and simmer for 1 minute till the oil rises to the surface. Cool and store.

Note: Sichuan sauce will keep for 1 month if there is sufficient oil covering the surface.

Vegetable Stock

Peel, wash and chop 1 onion, ½ medium carrot, 2-3 inches celery stalk and 2-3 garlic cloves. Place in a non-stick pan with 1 bay leaf, 5-6 peppercorns, 2-3 cloves and 5 cups of water and bring to a boil. Lower heat and simmer for 15 minutes and strain. Cool and store in a refrigerator till further use.

White Sauce

To make the white sauce, melt 2 tablespoons butter in a heavy-bottomed non-stick pan and stir in 2 tablespoons refined flour. Cook for five to six minutes over low heat till fragrant. Whisk in 2 cups milk till smooth. Cook for four to five minutes, stirring continuously, till the sauce thickens. Add salt to taste and ½ teaspoon white pepper powder and mix well. Strain the sauce.

Makes 2 cups

Glossary

English	Hindi
Almonds	Badam
Basil	Tulsi
Bay leaf	Tej patta
Black peppercorns	Kali mirch
Bottle gourd	Lauki
Button mushrooms	Khumb
Capsicum	Shimla mirch
Caraway seeds	Shahi jeera
Cardamom	Elaichi
Chickpeas	Kabuli chana
Cinnamon	Dalchini
Cloves	Laung
Fresh coriander	Hara dhania
Cottage cheese	Paneer
Fresh cream	Malai
Cumin seeds	Jeera
Dried fenugreek leaves	Kasoori methi
Dried red chillies	Sookhi lal mirch
Fennel seeds	Saunf

English	Hindi
Fenugreek seeds	Methi dana
Fresh parsley	Ajmoda
Lotus roots	Bhein
Pear	Naspati
Pineapple	Annanas
Pine nuts	Chilgoza
Pistachio	Pista
Pomegranate	Anar
Prawns	Jheenga
Raisins	Kishmish
Saffron	Kesar
Spinach	Palak
Gram, Bengal split	Chana dal
Spring onion greens	Hare pyaaz ki pattiyan
Sweetcorn kernels	Makai ke dane
Vinegar	Sirka
Walnuts	Akhrot